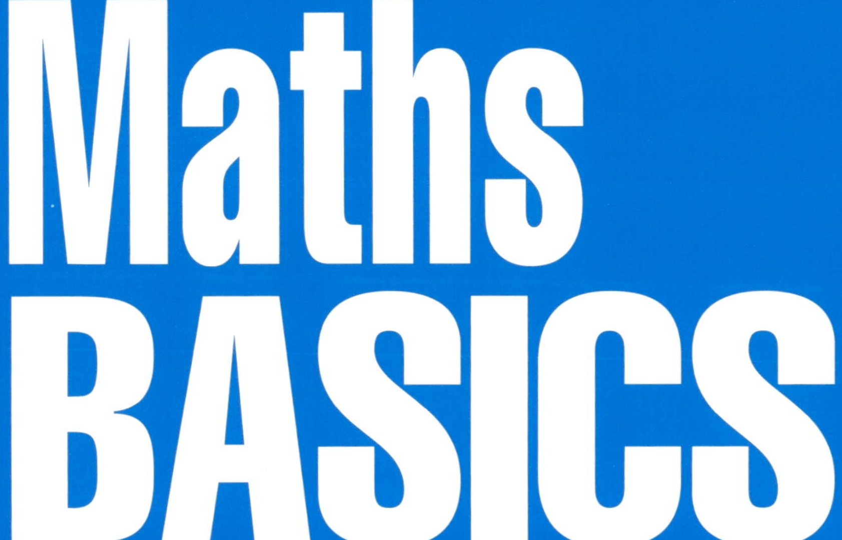

Contents

How to use this book

Numeracy Basics helps you to help your child practise many important basic skills covered in the *National Numeracy Strategy* and *National Curriculum*.

Each book is divided into *30 units* of work which focus on *one clear* objective.

Most of the units are designed using the same easy-to-follow *key features*. In some cases these features are combined into one activity, offering further practice where appropriate.

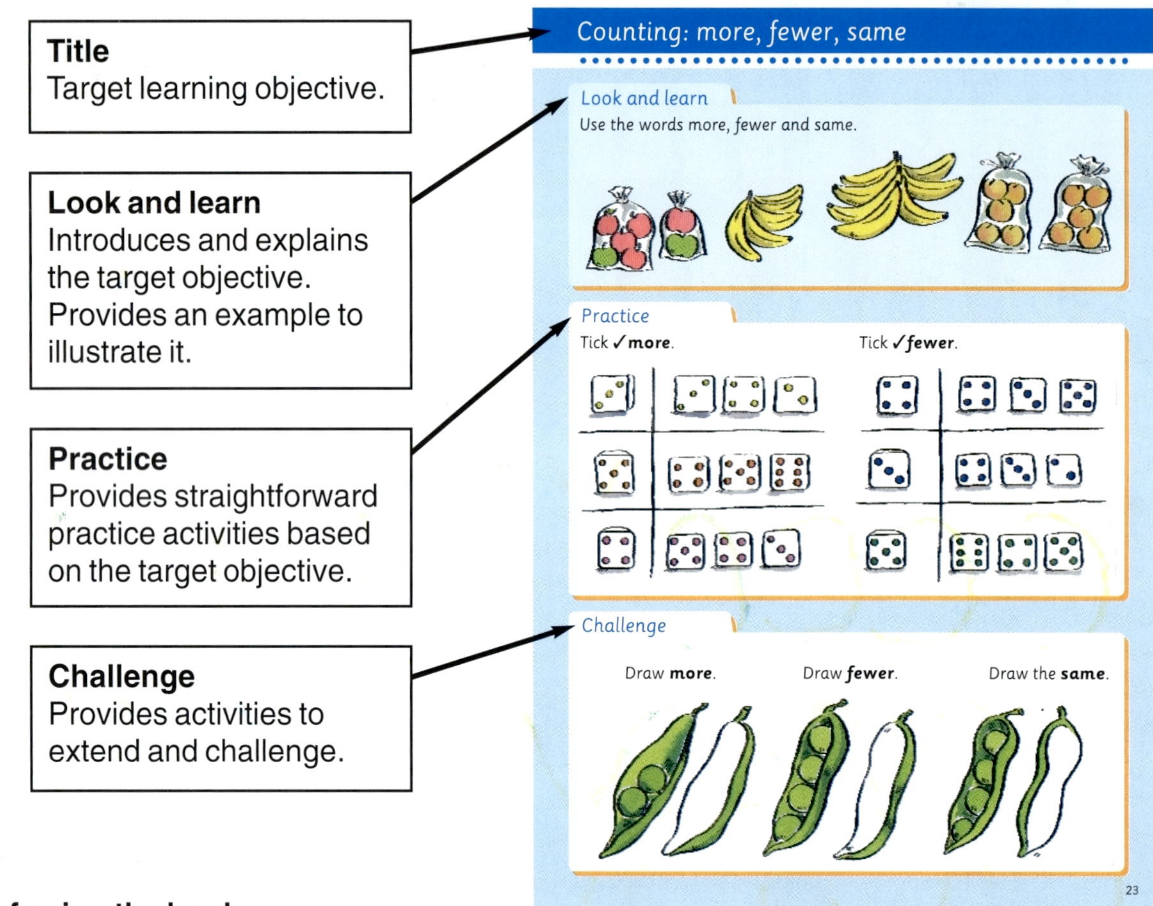

Suggested way of using the book

- It is suggested that your child works systematically through the book.
- Try tackling one unit per week.
- Read through and discuss the *Look and learn* section with your child to make sure the key objective is understood.
- Help your child get started on the Practice section.
- After this, your child can start to work fairly independently through the page, but will need further support and encouragement.
- The answers are supplied at the end of the book for checking each unit on its completion.

Enjoy the book!

Patterns: straight and curved lines

Look and learn

Trace over these **straight lines** and **curved lines**.

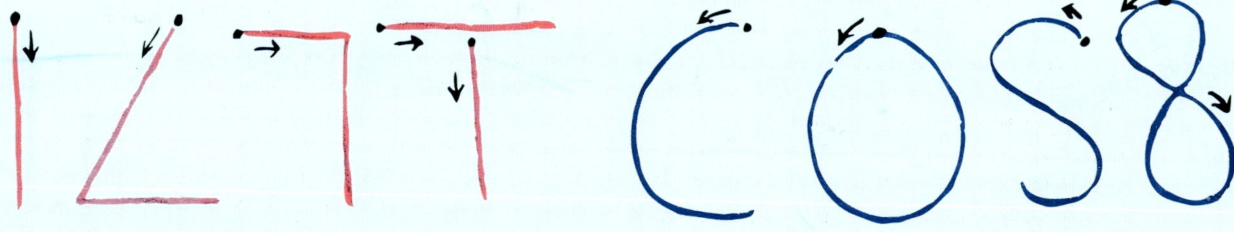

Practice

Trace over these.

Challenge

Trace over these.

Copying and continuing patterns

Look and learn

Some patterns go on and on.

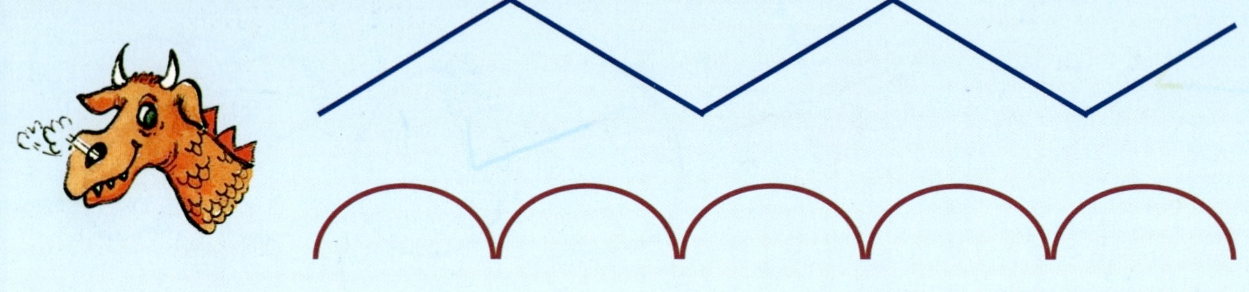

Practice

Complete these patterns.

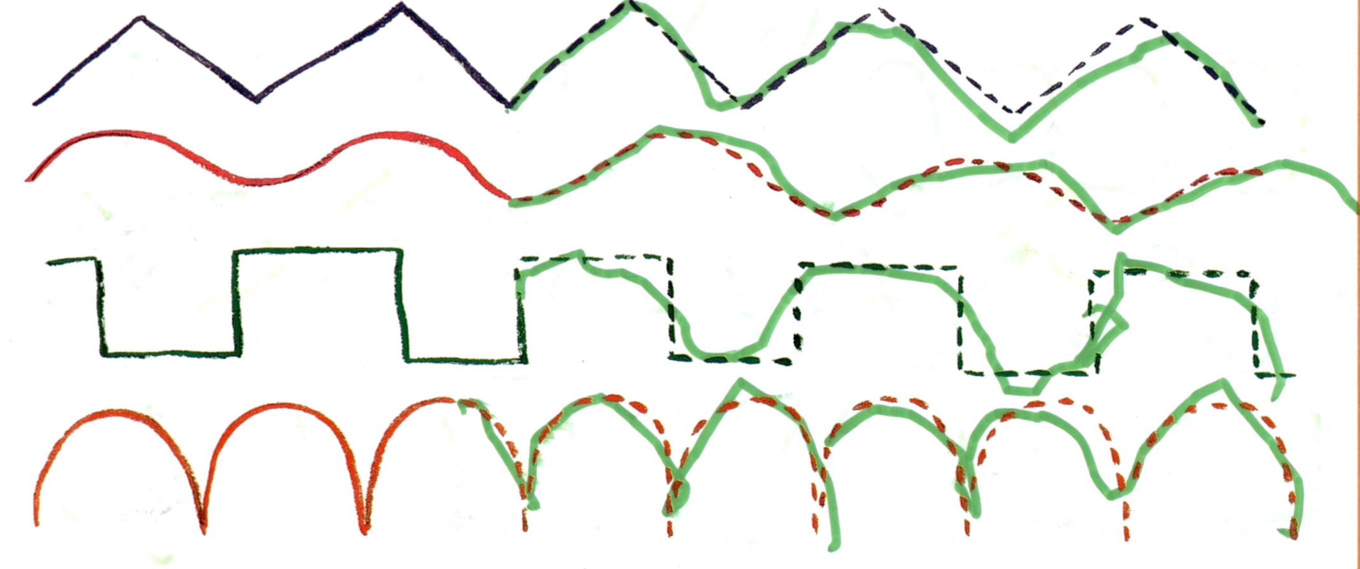

Challenge

Complete these patterns.

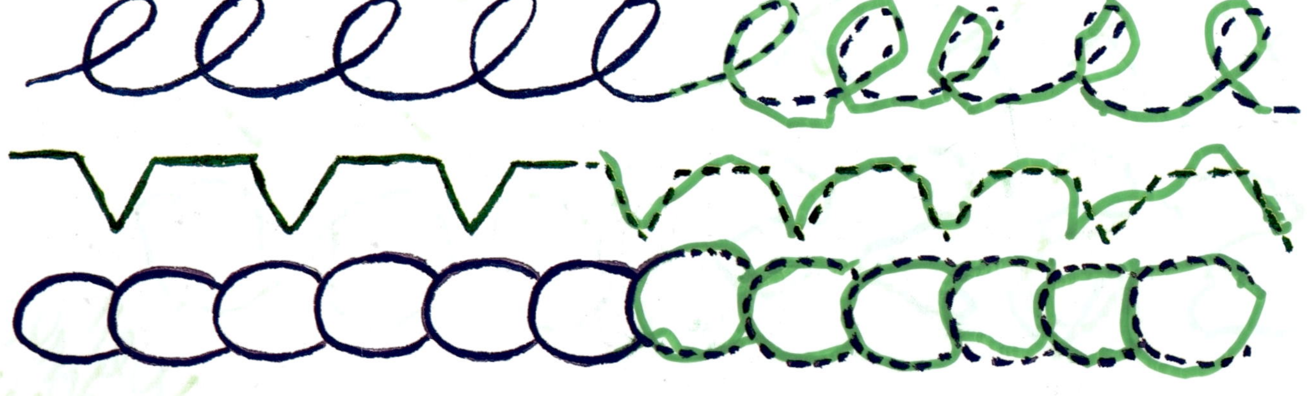

Look and learn

Your child needs to recognise shapes that are the same.

Practice

Find and colour the pairs of flowers.

Challenge

Find and colour the hidden shape in each set.

Look and learn

Your child needs to know which words describe sizes.

Practice

Tick ✓ the largest.

Tick ✓ the smallest.

Challenge

Join up the cats in order of size.

Join up the fish in order of size.

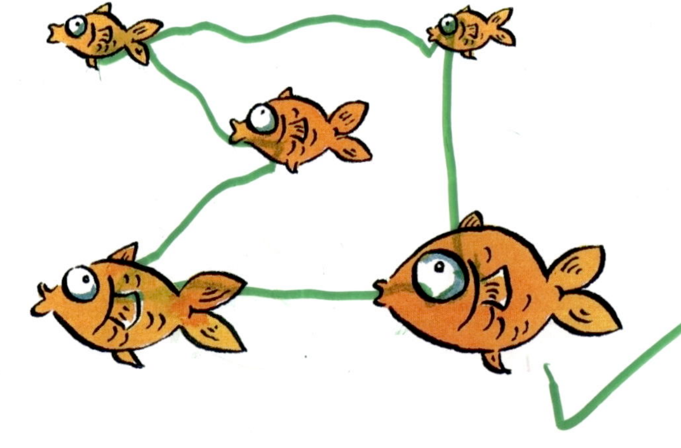

Look and learn

Show your child how to write the numbers:

0 1 2 3 4

Practice

Join the numbers to the sets with a line.

Challenge

Cross the odd one out in each set.

Writing numbers: **0, 1, 2, 3 and 4**

Look and learn

Practice writing these numbers.

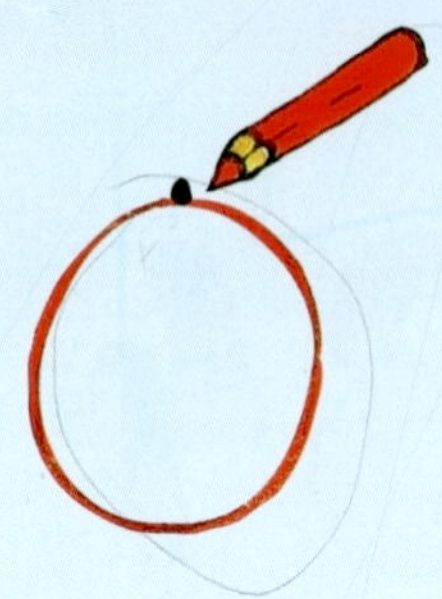

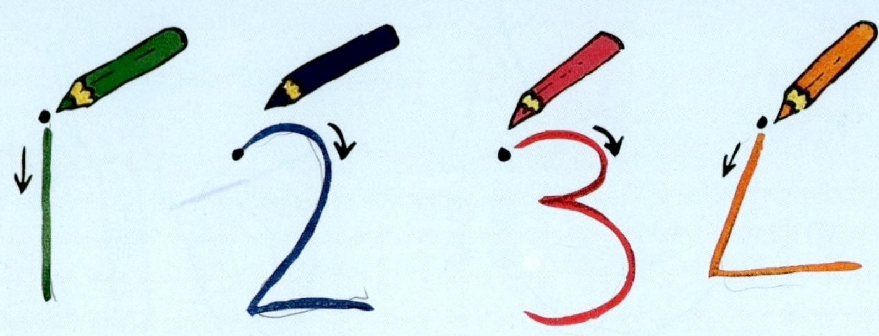

Practice

Trace over the numbers.

0 0 0 0 0 0 0 0 0 0 0 0

1 1 1 1 1 1 1 1 1 1 1 1

2 2 2 2 2 2 2 2 2 2 2 2

3 3 3 3 3 3 3 3 3 3 3 3

4 4 4 4 4 4 4 4 4 4 4 4

Challenge

Draw spots to match the numbers. Trace over the numbers.

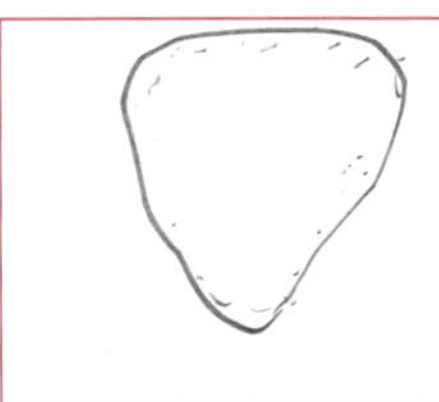

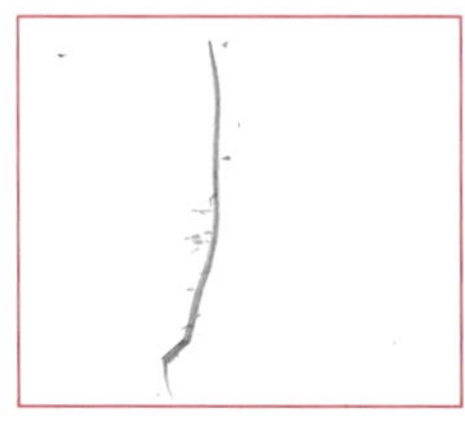

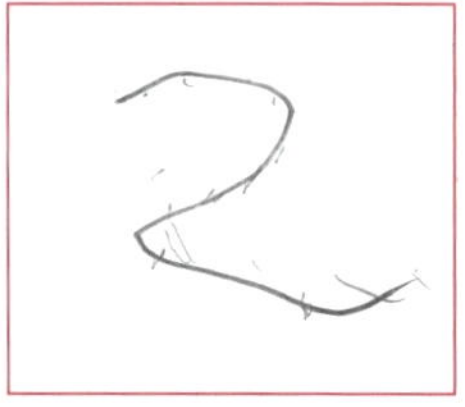

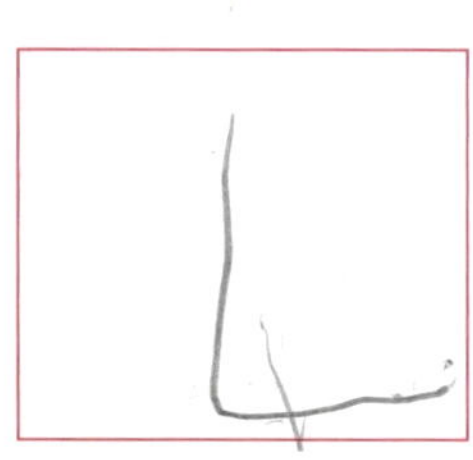

Look and learn

Show your child how to write these numbers.

3 4 5 6

Practice

Join the numbers to the sets with a line.

Challenge

Cross the odd one out in each set.

Shape: recognising common shapes

Look and learn

Your child needs to recognise common shapes.

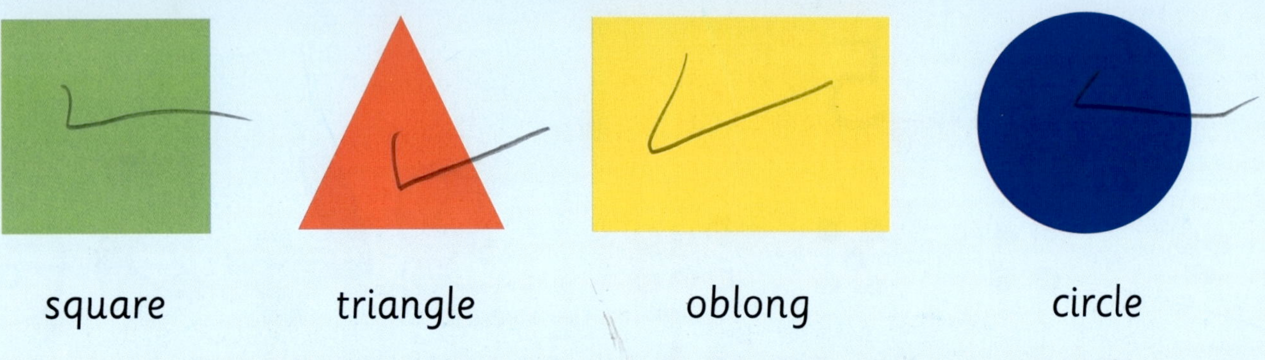

square triangle oblong circle

Practice

Colour the shapes in the picture to match the shapes above.

Challenge

Copy the shapes, then colour them in.

Measures: comparing lengths

Look and learn

Your child needs to be able to compare lengths.

tall taller tallest short shorter shortest

Practice

Tick ✓ the tallest in each group. Tick ✓ the smallest in each group.

Challenge

Tick ✓ the missing rod.

Look and learn

Ask your child to use pennies to show 5p.

Practice

Count the pennies and write the number in the purses.

Challenge

Colour the correct label.

Counting: numbers to **6**

Look and learn

Count the spots and say the numbers.

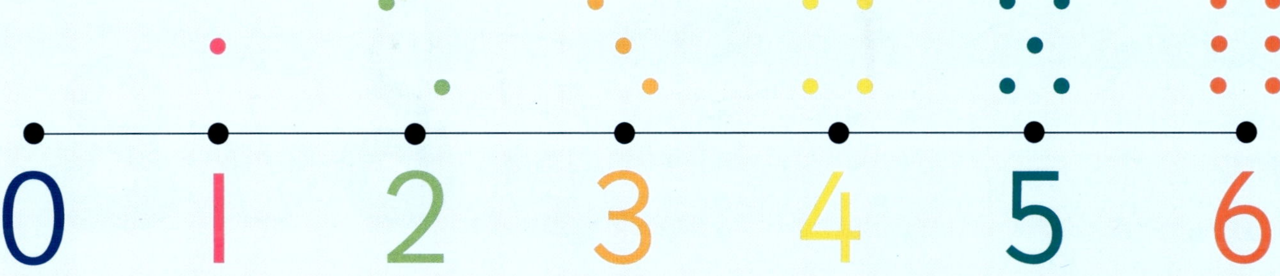

Practice

Count the objects in the boxes and draw a line to the correct number.

Challenge

Draw the correct number of balls in each sack.

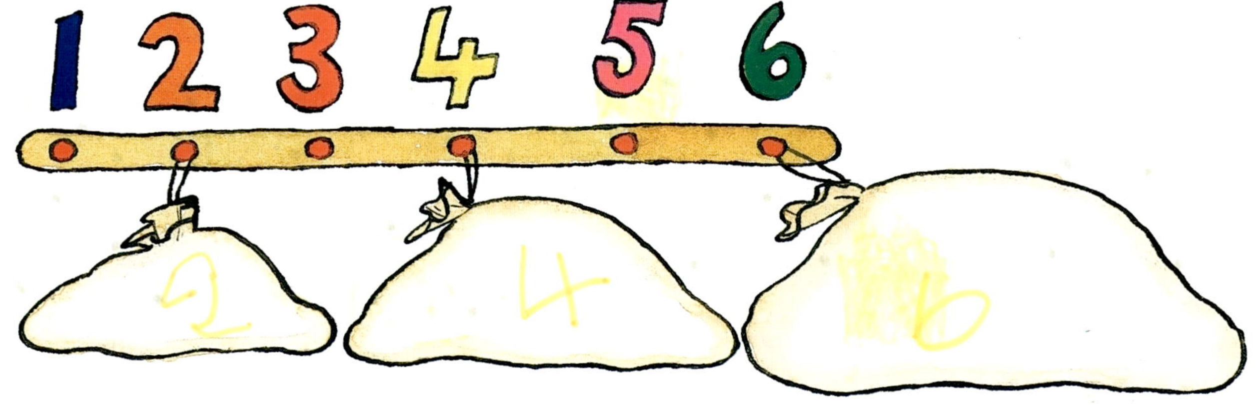

Counting: numbers 5 to **8**

Look and learn

Show your child how to write the numbers:

5 6 7 8

5678

Practice

Join the numbers to the sets.

Challenge

Draw spots on the t-shirts to equal the number below each picture.

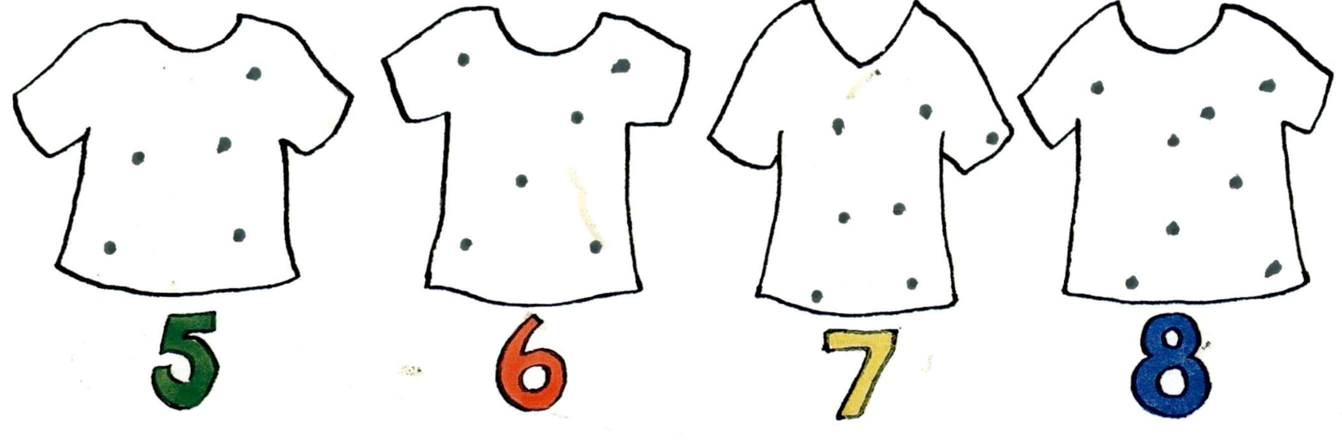

3D shapes

Look and learn

Show your child that moving an object does not make it a different shape.

The same shape in different positions.

Practice

Cross the odd shape out.

Challenge

Draw a line to join the shapes that match.

Look and learn

Your child needs to be able to compare and order lengths.

Practice

Colour the **longest**.

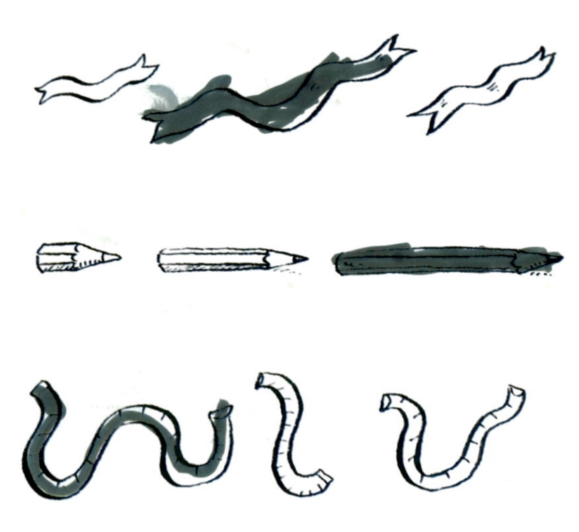

Colour the **shortest**.

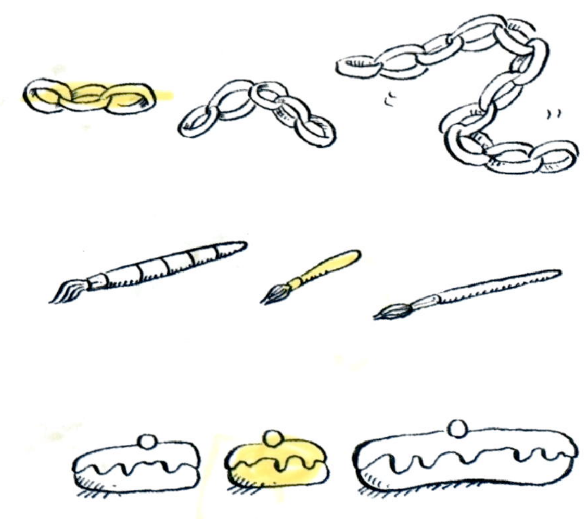

Challenge

Join the objects that are the same size.

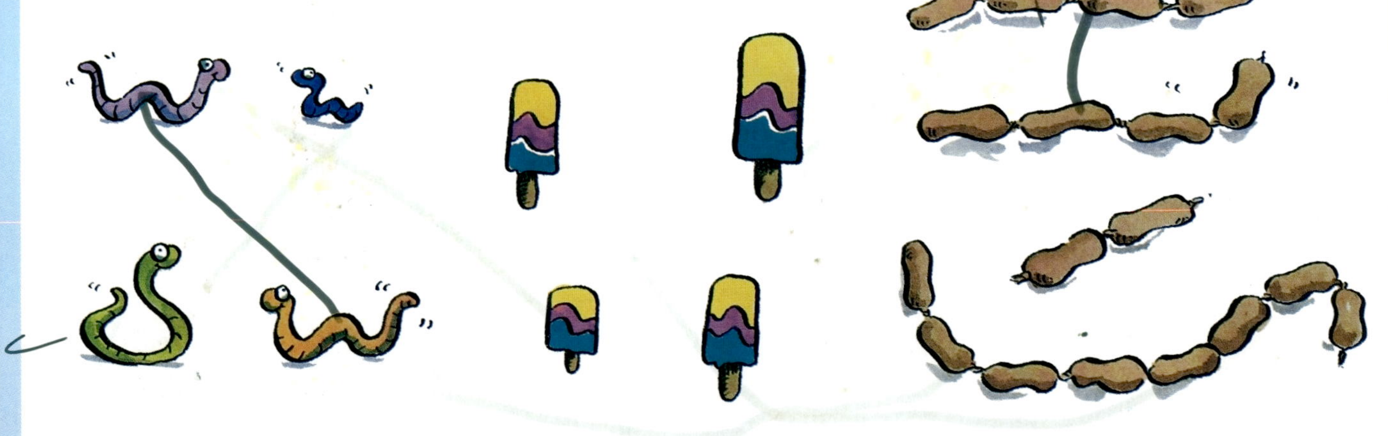

Look and learn

Give your child a small number and ask for one more.

 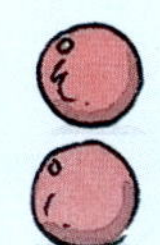   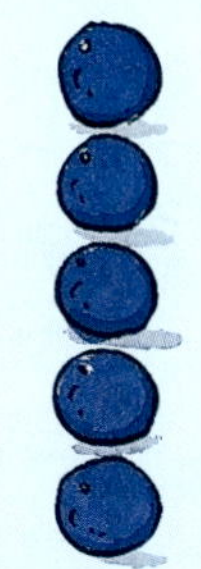

Practice

Draw **one more** in each box.

    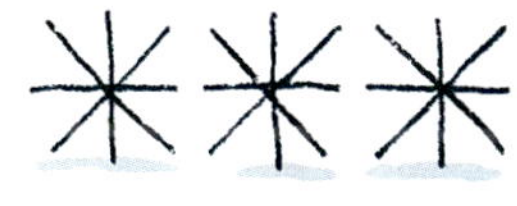 

 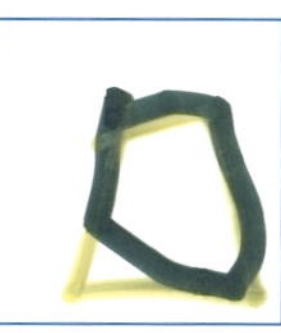     

Challenge

Draw **one more** ball.
Write the number.

 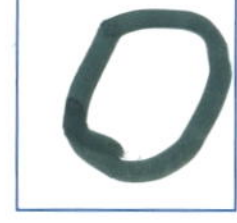  

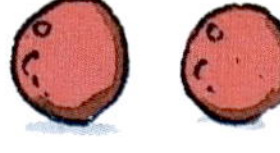 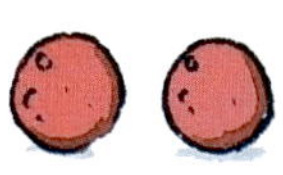  

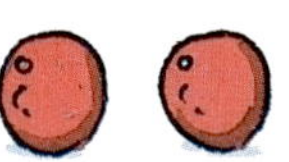  

Draw **one more** leg.
Write the number.

Writing numbers 5, 6 and 7

Look and learn

Practise writing these numbers.

Practice

Trace over these.

5 5 5 5 5 5 5 5 5 5 5 5

6 6 6 6 6 6 6 6 6 6 6 6

7 7 7 7 7 7 7 7 7 7 7 7

Challenge

Draw spots on each flag to equal the numbers.

Writing numbers 8, 9 and 10

Look and learn

Try writing these numbers.

Practice

Trace over these.

8 8 8 8 8 8 8 8 8

9 9 9 9 9 9 9 9 9

10

Challenge

Draw the correct number of spots on each ladybird.

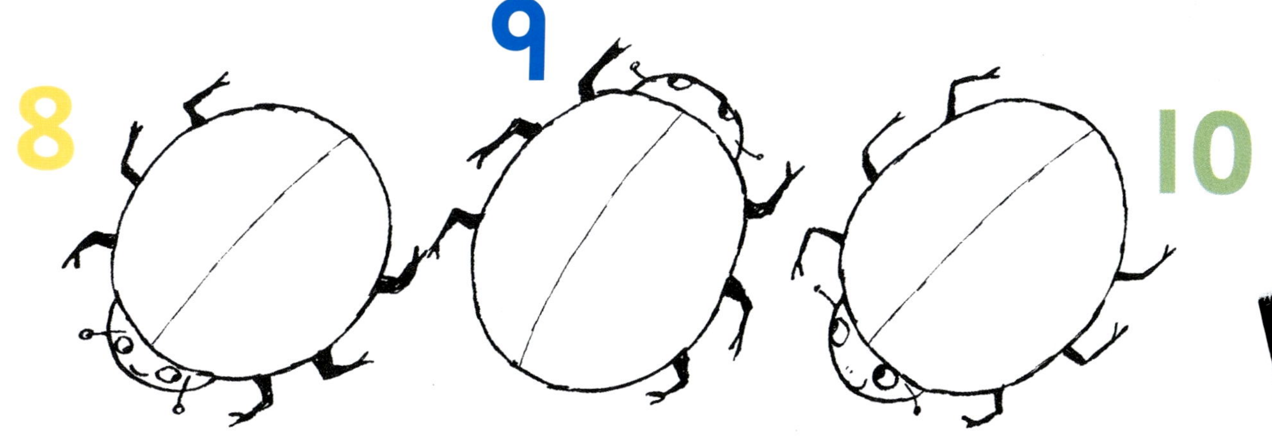

Shape: colour patterns

Look and learn

Your child needs to recognise simple patterns.

Practice

Colour the shapes to continue the patterns.

Challenge

Continue drawing the two shapes in the same patterns.

Comparing sizes

Look and learn

Your child needs to recognise things that are the same size.

Practice

Circle the objects that are the same size.

Challenge

Find which worms are the same size. Colour them.

Coins: recognising 1 and 2p coins

Look and learn

Talk about 1p and 2p coins.

Practice

Cross the odd one out in each purse.

Challenge

Tick ✓ the purses with 4p in them.

Counting: more, fewer, same

Look and learn

Talk about these pictures. Use the words **more**, **fewer** and **same**.

Practice

Tick ✓**more**.

Tick ✓**fewer**.

Challenge

Draw **more**.

Draw **fewer**.

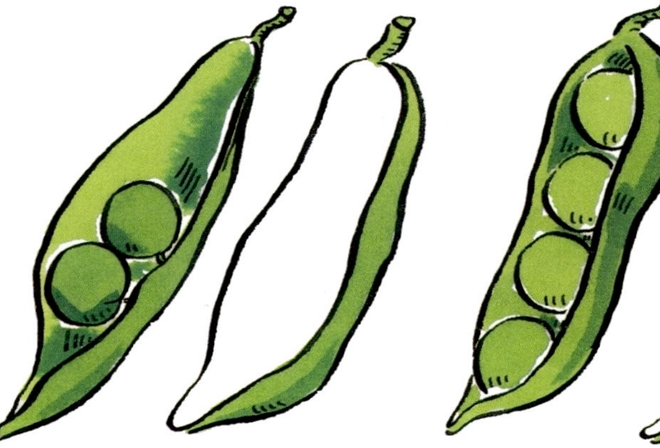

Draw the **same**.

Counting: same number

Look and learn

Your child needs to recognise when things are the same.

same

same

Practice

Tick ✓ the **same**.

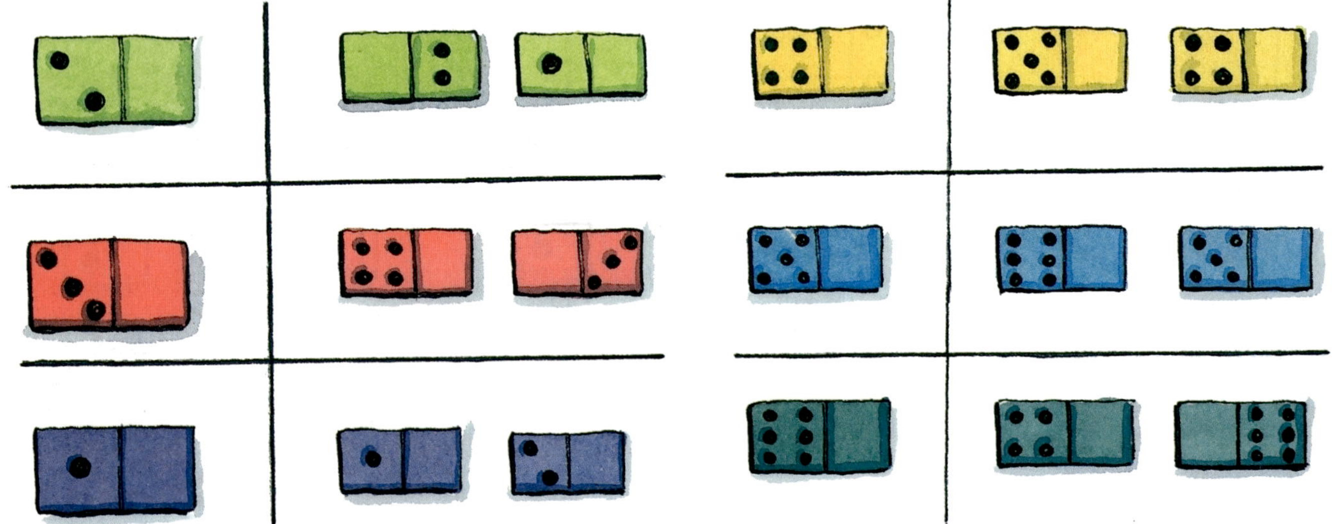

Challenge

Tick ✓ the **same**.

Look and learn

Look carefully at these shapes. Copy them.

Practice

Draw and colour the matching shapes.

Challenge

Finish drawing these shapes.

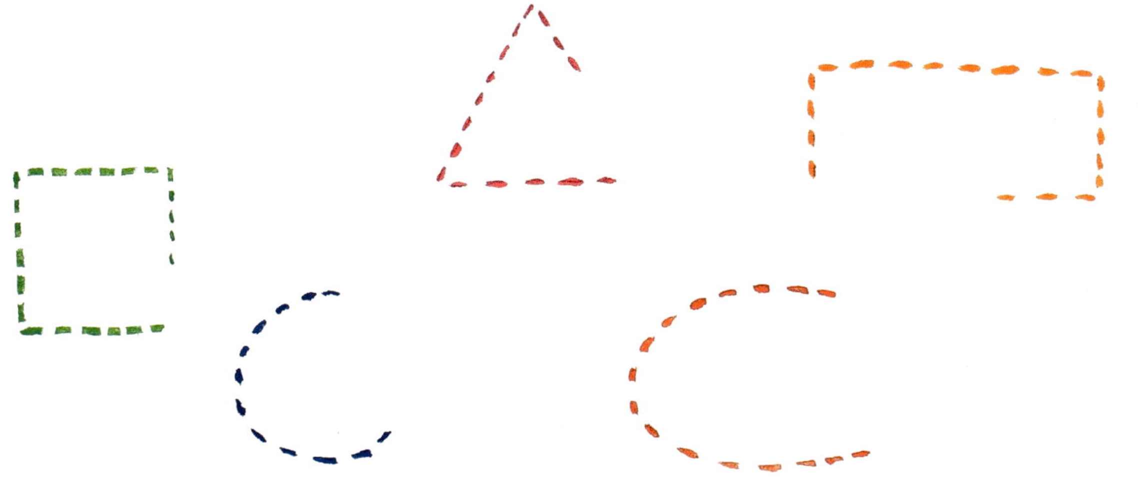

Look and learn

We do many things in a certain order.

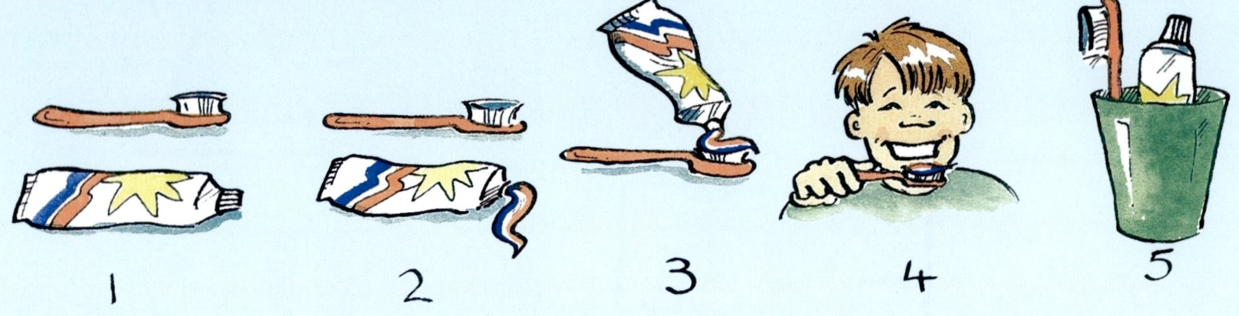

Practice

Write the numbers 1, 2, 3, 4 to show what happens next.

Challenge

Tick ✓ what you do in the morning.

Ordering numbers

Look and learn

Numbers have an order.

Practice

Join these up in order.

Challenge

Draw the missing peas.

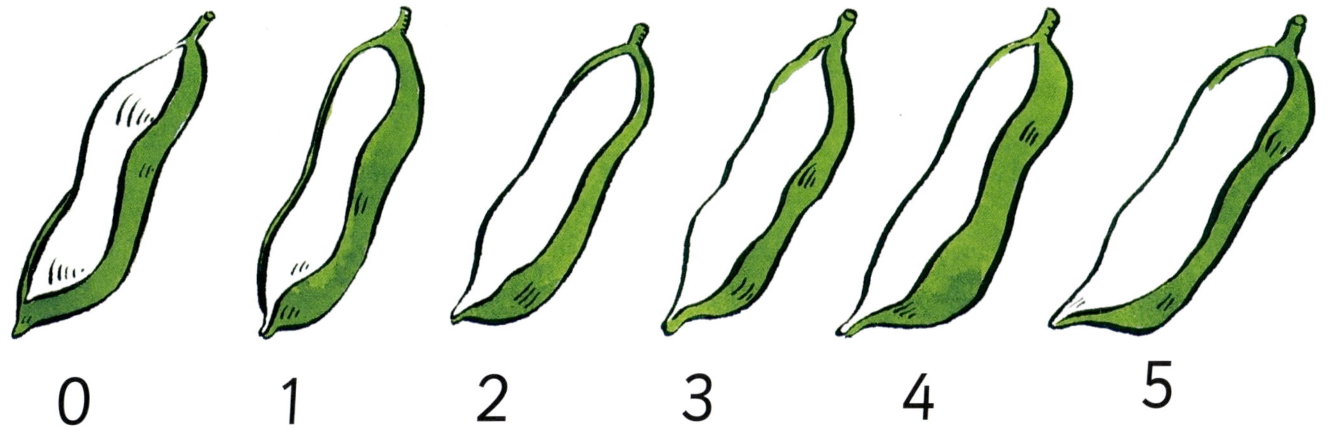

Adding

Look and learn

Put together small amounts to demonstrate adding.

Practice

Write the number.

Challenge

Add up the dots on each of the dominoes and draw a line to the pair with a matching total.

Taking away

Look and learn

Show your child how to take **1** away.

Practice

Take away **1**. What is left?

Take away **2**. What is left?

Challenge

Take away **1**p.

Take away **2**p.

2D shapes

Look and learn

Read the names of the shapes to your child.

square

triangle

rectangle

circle

Practice

Cross the odd one out.

Challenge

Colour the **squares**.

Colour the **triangles**.

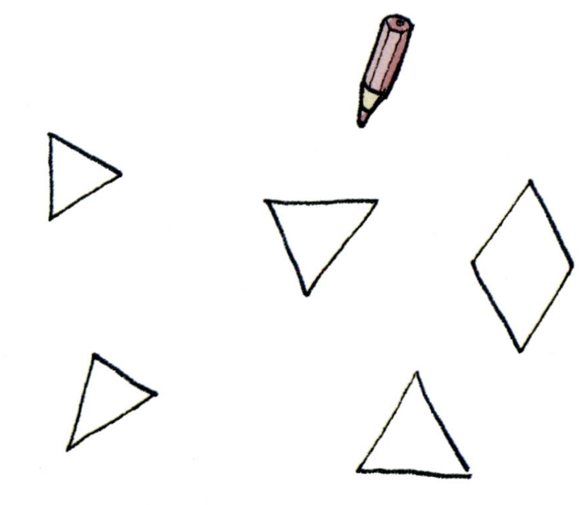

Time: night and day

Look and learn

Talk about the things that happen at night and during the day.

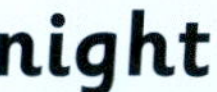

Practice

Cross the odd one out in each group of three.

night

Challenge

Circle the odd things.

Money: recognising coins

Look and learn

Talk about the **shape**, **size** and **colour** of coins.

Practice

Cross the odd one out.

Challenge

Match the coins.